Getting It Out There: PR and Social Media for Writers

Nancy Gideon

Getting It Out There: PR and Social Media for Writers

Budgeting Time and Money / Branding, What's in a Name?

Printed in United States of America

Ivy Tower Imprint

Wise Words Publishing
Swartz Creek. MI 48473
www.wisewordspublishing.com

For More Information

CarolToppCPA.com and TaxesForWriters.com,
<u>Business Tips and Taxes for Writers</u> by Carol Topp.

A Business Plan for Self-Published Authors
(www.suite101.com/cntent/a-business-plan-for-self-published-authors-a328587, Aneeta Sundararaj

Acknowledgments

Thanks to JoAnn Ross, Cassandra Clare, James Patterson and Sherrilyn Kenyon for setting such good examples, and to all the other authors mentioned for getting out there in a unique way.

Table of Contents

Budgeting Time and Money

Writers come into a publishing career with some strange misconceptions. I know I did. We sometimes think that becoming a published author is as simple as having a computer, a printer and correct postage to mail in our submissions. For me, it was. Actually, it was with a typewriter. I wrote longhand into a notebook, typed up that historical romance novel and sent it off to New York. It sold! I became a published author. The hard part was over. Now, all I had to do was sit back and wait for the money to roll in.

I waited.

And waited.

More books sold. More waiting.

Where was that pot of gold and early retirement the illusion of being a writer had promised me?

What I discovered between that first sale and my first royalty check was a surprising fact about a having and holding onto a writing career: Writing is a business.

I was an English major (you do the math!). I never took business classes. I was going to make my living on creativity alone. Think it up, send it out, get paid, live well. That was the entire scope of my plan. A very simple plan. A very short-sighted plan.

Writing, I learned, was the simple part. Maintaining a career wasn't about free-range creativity, it was about business. The business of writing.

If all you want to do is write for the sheer, fulfilling joy of writing, good for you! It's a wonderful way to express yourself. If you want to share your work with others so it might enrich and entertain them, all the better. If you want to make a living from it, you need to learn some cold, analytical (Oh no! Math is involved!) facts about turning that lovely, free-flowing hobby into a paying and potentially self-sustaining career.

The business of writing involves investing and channeling your time and money *before* you start making it. And like any new business, you need to approach it smartly with a plan for success.

A Business Plan: Don't leave home without it!

Think developing a business plan is just for those Fortune 500 folk with companies and stock options? Wrong. YOU are your own writing company, and creating a solid, well thought out business plan can be the key that takes you from struggling hobbyist to successful author.

When do you need a business plan? Now. If you're reading this, you're considering the long-term results of a writing future. Approach that future wisely by developing a clear, upfront vision of what you expect to do for, and reap from, your writing business. Begin by carefully reviewing the following 12-steps (I love a 12-step program), answering the questions each step poses as to how it applies to your unique situation, and formulating those responses into your personal plan for setting up and sustaining a writing career. Remember, you can't "Get It Out There" unless you have it first.

1) <u>Identify Your Product:</u> What are you planning to produce? Fiction? Short stories? Plays? Articles? Give a detailed description, i.e. contemporary romance fiction of approximately 55,000 words; sci-fi/fantasy short stories; action/adventure screenplays; self-help articles relating to ADHD in adults and children.

2) <u>Develop a Mission Statement:</u> Sounds scary, but it's really just common sense. What is your purpose for what you plan to write? To entertain? To educate? What makes your product special? (Insert what you learned creating your Author Brand here.) Why will your product be successful? Is it something you love to read? Something that follows or

pre-guesses marketing trends? Something readers are snapping off the shelves? Or something new and wildly unique?

3) <u>Who are your Customers?</u> What do they want? What are they looking for? How will you provide it with your product? Identifying your target audience will determine the venues you choose and determine the hook you'll develop to pull them in.

4) <u>What is your Marketing Plan?</u> How are you going to get your product to the reader? On the shelves? On line? On your own? What niche does it fit into? Where can it be found by its audience?

5) <u>How much Start-Up Capital do you have available?</u> It takes more than pen and ink. How much time and money do you have to *realistically* invest in your writing career? Do you already have a primary income yourself, or a secondary income from a spouse or significant other? Are you already working full time in another area? Do you have the money in hand to buy all that you need and provide for expenses as they come up, or will you have to pay-as-you-go?

6) <u>What will it take to Launch your Writing Career?</u> Do you have a designated writing

space? The tools to produce your product—In actual materials such as a computer, software, printer, toner, Internet access, desk/work area, domain name, website, office supplies? Or intangibles like knowledge and skill development, i.e. writing classes, organization fees, contests, conferences?

7) <u>How Do You Plan to Promote Your Product?</u> Social networking? Book events? Interviews and speaking engagements? Through friends and people you know? Advertising? Will you need a publicist or a virtual assistant? How are you going to reach out to your target audience and connect with them? Do a reality check for both available time and money.

8) <u>How Much Money will you Need to Meet your Goals?</u> Where will you get it? How can you scale back to make do with what you have? Here's where the next section on creating your budget comes into play.

9) <u>How Much Time will it take to Establish Yourself?</u> An overnight sensation? Realistically, it takes four to five books to gain a steady audience. What's the minimum amount of time your project requires on a daily, weekly, monthly basis to complete it and keep it going? How much writing time?

How much social media time? Look for extra pockets of time. Can you get up earlier? Can you do your social media on your lunch hour? Create a timeline from inception to release for your product, and carry it through its promotion. Adjust it to fit your realistic time and money availability.

10) Get your Professional Posse In Place: Who you gonna call for help? Make a list of those advisors that you need on speed dial. Your critique group. Your agent. A literary attorney. An accountant. Your computer guru. Your writing peers online and on loops. Printers and designers for your promotional materials. These are your go-to individuals for assistance, whether you're using them now or will in the future. Make a list and keep it updated to save yourself time and energy when a situation, either planned or unexpected, arises.

11) Develop a Contingency Plan: We love it when a plan comes together, but sometimes it doesn't happen smoothly. Consider in advance what you'll do if you hit road blocks. How will you deal with setbacks and delays? Life gets in the way. What will you do if family, financial or health issues rear their ugly

heads? How will you handle rejections or writer's block if they slow down your success timeline? Will you be able to carry on if the money slows or stops all together? Can you adjust your schedule around unexpected illness or obligations by either extending your deadlines or creating emergency pockets of extra time? Running these worst-case scenarios in advance changes their untimely arrival from total devastation into a survivable inconvenience.

12) <u>When is it in your Best Interest to Let Go?</u>
Sometimes that best laid plan just doesn't work out no matter how hard you try. Sometimes you just can't deliver. How will you know when it's time to shift gears or just walk away? Don't hold on to a plan longer than necessary when it becomes obvious it's going to take you down with it. Reevaluate frequently. Take stock of your options. What's your bottom line? What do you need to realize from your returns, both financially and professionally? These are the hard questions. If your "What's in it for me?" needs are not being fulfilled, you need to have an exit strategy in place. Where will you go if your current plan doesn't work out? Back to full

time work while you explore new avenues? To a new agent, editor, publisher? To self-publishing? Knowing how you'll survive the zombie writing apocalypse if it comes will guarantee you're a survivor. It doesn't hurt to have a creative nest egg in place should you ever need it.

The B-Word: Budget!

Budgeting doesn't have to be a dirty word. Think of it simply as a way to keep track of income and expenses: What's coming in and what's going out.

Every author dreams of supporting themselves with their craft. Getting a good budget in place is vital for a writer because their finances are unpredictable at best. The object is to set one up, then see if you can work comfortably within it before making that leap to dependency on your writer's income. Sorry, math is involved.

Step One: What's coming in?

Determine your available household income. Include yours, your spouse or significant other's, and other sources such as side jobs, dividends, interest, etc.

- If your income is stable, use your minimum monthly income from the previous 12-months as an average.
- If your income fluctuates, use an average of your previous 3-12 months. Don't go by the highest months.
- If your income is seasonal, average all 12 months.

You can use the amounts from set contracts to figure into your income, but make it realistic. Never count on royalties to make up the difference.

Step Two: Figure up your expenses.
- Start with your fixed expenses that you have every month: mortgage or rent, car payment, insurance, loans or debt installments, taxes. These amounts won't change from month to month and are easily averaged
- Total your fluctuating expenses over the course of six months to a year: groceries, gas, utilities, subscriptions like magazines, newspaper, gym, entertainment, then average them.

Step Three: Subtract expenses from your income.
This should net you a positive or a negative number. If it's a negative number, find where the

greatest deficiencies are then make the necessary adjustments to your spending/saving habits. Even a small change in your spending can influence a negative in your income.

To help make cuts in your spending, divide your expenses into things you have to have to survive (your needs) such as rent, food, utilities; and those things you like but can live without (your wants) such as cable, subscriptions, memberships, entertainments. When income is limited, the needs come first. Your wants come from the surplus. If there's a significant shortage, temporarily cancel services you don't need until you can afford them again. Debts come before wants. Don't let your bills go unpaid.

Step Four: Balance your budgeted income.

If there's a monthly surplus, save it in a specified income account. If you get a bonus, a tax refund or an unexpected royalty check, resist the desire to spend it. Put it in that special account earmarked for the budget.

If there's a monthly deficit, draw from that income account to tide you over.

If the months you're short outweigh your ability to compensate for them, start making those cuts, firmly and consistently. Consider meeting with a financial planner or a debt counselor.

Living solely off a writing income is difficult and requires a lot of self-discipline. Make sure you're financially secure before you quit your day job. You'll want to set up two accounts, one for your writing income (from which you pay yourself) and one you save from (where you deposit you checks). Pay yourself a weekly, bi-weekly or monthly salary based on your budgeted income so that even if there are monthly highs and lows, your personal income remains steady and dependable. Transfer only your pre-determined salary into your writing account to meet your budget needs, even when you take in a higher amount.

The Cost of Your Writing Career

Most of your writing expenses are negotiable. Where you draw the line between need and want is up to you. Whether you fire up your laptop on the corner of the dining room table or rent a writer's studio, you're still an author. You can do research on the Internet if you can't afford an excursion to Ireland. You can attend a writers group at your local bookstore or library if you can't budget in the dues to a national organization or their pricy conferences. You can pay thousands of dollars for a professional to develop your website and update it for you, or you can learn the basics to put your own up. Do the best professional job you can afford to do in all areas of your writing career. These are business expenses and should be treated as investments in your writing future.

Your cost of doing business as a writer can be broken down into three categories:

- Start-up expenses: your computer, writing and business software, Internet connection, printer, domain name, website development, author photo, business cards, business bank account, desk, chair, organization fees, conferences or classes to gain the necessary skills, and if you're doing self-publishing, any necessary business licenses, copyright and registration fees, ISBN/EAN costs, costs involved in production of your product: editing, cover art, setup fees, formatting, etc.

- Office supplies: paper, ink, toner, sticky notes, mailer envelopes, postage, notebooks, files, rubber bands, pens, paperclips, etc.

- Marketing expenses: advertisements, promotional materials i.e. bookmarks, flyers, Romance Trading Cards, copies of your own books, giveaways, book trailers, promotional appearances or fan conventions, trade magazines, contest fees, etc.

A Taxing Issue: The IRS

The only certainties in life are death and taxes. If you're making any type of livelihood from your writing, the government is going to want their cut of it.

The Internal Revenue Service requires you to differentiate between writing as a hobby and writing for profit. If you want to write off your expenses, you need to be able to prove that your writing is a legitimate business. Aside from making money three out of five years, you need to document that your writing expenses are ordinary (common and accepted in the profession) and necessary (money that needs to be spent in the operation of your business).

Bookkeeping is an important part of the business of writing. You need to not only list your income, you need to be able to justify your expenses if audited, and the best way to do that is to establish the habit of identifying and tracking those expenses. Make it a practice of keeping all receipts that have anything to do with your writing, even if you're not sure they are allowable. Make a note on the receipt regarding how it relates to writing. For example, if you go out to dinner for the purpose of doing an interview, write that on the receipt, listing who you spoke to. If asked the purpose of the meal three years from now, without that reminder, you might not be able to recall the reason. If you go to a film to study layering and character development, make a note. If you take a trip to a winery because you plan to base a book or an article around a vintner, jot down the working title of the book or potential source for publication. Don't assume you'll remember. Don't assume you can't use it. I've written off a ticket to a magic show, a rain forest jaunt, the cost of processing a roll of film, a haunted walking tour of the Garden District in New Orleans. And I've looked at an invoice for $49.98 from Best Buy and haven't had a clue what it was for. Just like with your works in progress, a backup is the only way to go. Keep the receipt and note the occasion.

Tracking your finances can be as simple as receipts in a shoebox (not recommended but better than nothing) or writing your expenses down on a sheet of paper listing date, item, reason for expenditure and cost and attaching an envelop to contain the receipt, credit card slip, invoice or bank statement. The downside is it's hard to tell without doing the math what your total is. You can also enter your expenses on a spreadsheet using Microsoft Excel which has columns that can be added, but the downside is the lack of space for detailing the reason for the expense and the inability to create a financial statement. It doesn't have to be pretty or high tech.

The important thing is developing a habit of saving everything that documents a writing expense in one place and consistent record keeping on either a weekly or monthly basis.

For Example

My first record-keeping system was basic, convenient, cheap and accurate. I still use it today. At the beginning of the new tax year, I make a trip to the office supply store to pick up a simple business bookkeeping spiral bound ledger sectioned off into months. I immediately label envelopes with the expense categories listed on the Schedule C form along with a few extras, i.e. Income, Advertising, Office Supplies, Office Equipment, Travel, Entertainment, Research, Postage, Dues and Subscriptions, Utilities. During the month, I tuck my receipts into the book, having noted on each one what it was for (Dinner with Critique group to brainstorm new RS, MMRWA meeting, Taxi from hotel to S&S for video interview, virus protector renewal, new business cards, book trailer for M by M, RT ad for H of S). At the end of the month, I list the expenses by date in the ledger and total them. Then I separate the receipts into the tax categories and total those on the facing page of the ledger. The totals should match. It's a good measure-twice-cut-once habit even if you are good at math. The monthly totals are added to a Year-to-Date column. Now you have your monthly expense total and a total for the tax categories, so you can tell in a glance where your money is going. There are also lines for your income and estimated tax payments, so you can subtract current expenses from income and figure out fairly accurately what your tax burden is to date.

Once they are tallied, the receipts go into the categorized envelopes where they are ready for a year-end totaling at tax time into my Turbo Tax program. Listing, sorting and totaling as you go eliminates chances of making errors or omissions and keeps you on top of your spending.

I also include my mileage in the ledger: date/purpose of trip/total miles.

No matter what system you use, use it! Keep it up to date and organized, and your tax experience will be so much more pleasant.

Important reminder: Do not co-mingle your personal and business finances! Keep them separate! Separate bank accounts and credit cards are preferred (the cost of setting those up is an allowable business expense, too!)

Your writing projects can start as a hobby but quickly grow into a business. Be prepared should your new business blossom overnight into a full-time endeavor or even a corporation. Speak to an accountant to find the best way to present your writing business to the government: as sole proprietor, as a corporation or an LLC (Limited Liability Company). There are advantages to each, so find out which is in your best interest.

Remember, your writing is a business. If you file a Schedule C, the state and federal government will expect you to behave as one . . . or penalize you for your failure to act as one. Once you're earning income, prepare to pay quarterly estimated taxes to both your State and the IRS. This is where your careful accounting comes in to play if anything on your returns comes in to question. It's a good idea to have a tax accountant/CPA who is familiar with the unique situation of writers go over your accounts, at least to get you started on the right foot (that visit to the accountant is a write off, too!) They can help you interpret tax forms and IRS lingo. If you get a letter from the IRS questioning your return or reported income, call in a professional.

There are plenty of tax deductions for writers, but use them wisely. Document them carefully and make sure you understand what they allow. Find out your obligations in the categories of inventory, sales tax, Social Security contributions and Self-employment tax.

Deductions are your friends. They chip away at that untaxed writing income and immediately reduce your tax burden. Know where to find them and how to use them. Here are some examples:

- Advertising: Here's where your promotional efforts pay off big time. This would apply to everything involved in getting your name out there: bookmarks, press photos, flyers, ads, giveaways (those cute temporary tattoos, inscribed pencils and pens, bumper stickers, door hangers), business cards, book trailers, blog and website design and maintenance, copies of your books that you give away or send to reviewers, and the printing, design and distribution costs of any promotional media . . . as long as you have receipts!

- Insurance: Only if you have no other health insurance available to you and are self-employed.

- Interest: i.e. interest accrued as you pay off your new computer

- Legal and professional: That visit to the accountant, to the tax or literary attorney. Your tax software, i.e. Turbo Tax

- <u>Rent or lease</u>: This is NOT your apartment or home rental. This would apply if you rent a separate space in which to conduct your writing business.

- <u>Repairs and Maintenance:</u> If it's electrical, it breaks down. Computer and printer repairs are the big ones.

- <u>Supplies:</u> Office supplies are those disposable things that you use up and replace (not to be confused with desk chairs and office lighting). Ink, toner, paper, ledger for bookkeeping, envelopes, sticky notes, folders, glass cleaner, canned air, etc.

- <u>Travel:</u> Another big ticket item if you go to conferences, conventions, out-of-town meetings or do on-site research. Expenses would include airfare, hotel, ground transportation, and parking. Don't forget to ask that cab driver for a receipt or keep the stub for the hotel shuttle.

- <u>Meals and Entertainment:</u> You can only write off a percentage of your meals, and they have to directly apply to the course and scope of your writing business. Meals while you're at a conference, convention or writers meeting. Dinners where writing is the main reason for gathering (here's where it's imperative to note who you were with and what you discussed!) Don't abuse or go overboard and not expect the IRS to question it. Taking your critique group to an All Nude Review or Fashion Week show are suspect unless your current or upcoming writing project directly involves All Nude Reviews or Fashion Week. Buying a round for the house, while generous, isn't necessarily deducible. When in doubt, save the receipts and get clarification from your accountant.

- Utilities: Only if you don't use the Business Use of Home deduction or if you're writing loft is a separate rental space.

- Other Expenses: Here's where you customize the uniqueness of being a writer. I routinely add 'Dues and Subscriptions' to cover conference and contest fees, membership dues to writing or research related organizations, industry trade or research books and magazines, 'Postage' for those overnight mailings or giveaway packages as well as stamps, 'business phone' if you have one dedicated strictly to business.

- Create a New Category: Anything that you believe might be an allowable expense unique to the profession.

20

There are certain Red Flags that the government watches for in your returns, some of them being Business Use of Home (make sure you can prove the space is dedicated exclusively to your writing business—not the corner of the dining room table), claiming losses for three out of five years, using incorrect forms or listing expenses on the wrong lines, extravagant amounts under the Meals and Entertainment section. And, of course, failure to pay quarterly estimated taxes is another big one they frown upon.

Your writing is your business. Not treating it as one can lead to other mistakes that can prove disastrous over time. Here's a Red Flag list of financial errors you don't want to make:

1. Failure to establish a budget and stick to it
2. Failure to keep accurate records of income and expenses
3. Failure to control your spending and getting too deeply in debt
4. Failure to keep personal and business finances separate
5. Failure to pay quarterly estimated tax payments
6. Failure to reconcile your bank accounts
7. Failure to repay your obligations promptly

8. Failure to back up your data. This applies to more than just your W-I-P.
9. Failure to understand the business aspects of the profession, i.e. contracts, taxes, potential earnings
10. Failure to invest in your business so it can grow, i.e. self-promotion, upgrading equipment/software, continuing professional education, reevaluating and diversifying

You don't want EPIC FAIL stamped on your writing future, so take the time to establish proper business habits and pay attention to the business of writing.

Accounting Software for Writers

There are some great software packages out there that are geared toward the needs of small businesses and freelance writers that are easy to use without the pricy overkill bells and whistles. Many of them offer a free trial, so give them a spin first to see if they'll work for you.

To help with your budget:

These FREE, secure tracking tools will automatically assist you with your budget by linking to your existing financial accounts: credit cards, bank accounts, investments so you can see what you're spending and where your money goes. Expenditures are automatically categorized and a budget is prepared for you. They track your investments, remind you when to pay your bills, and even show you where you can save money.

- Mint.com
- Bundle.com

To handle your accounting:

These packages will help small businesses/freelance writers organize their finances, categorize their expenses and prepare a Profit & Loss statement so you can assess the financial health of your writing business.

- Quicken.Intuit.com (small business version of QuickBooks/$99)
- Freshbooks.com (also does time tracking and invoicing/starts at $19.95 per month
- Outright.com ($9.95 per month)
- Microsoft Office Accounting Express (Integrates with other Office programs, E-bay, processes orders/FREE)

Time Is Money!

It's easy for writers to overlook one of their biggest assets or expenses—their TIME. YOU are your product. Your TIME has value. If you aren't actively pursuing the business of writing, you aren't earning money. The book won't write itself. If you don't have something to sell, then budget, expenses, and accounting won't matter.

Time is the resource most frequently abused or unrecognized in our profession. We waste it, misuse, give it away, cry about not having enough of it. The fact is, we think nothing of budgeting our money but are surprised by the notion of budgeting our time.

Whenever we're at the keyboard, we're putting money in our business bank. When we're doing our job, we're investing in the stability of our business. But the business of writing is more than just words on paper. We know that. It involves expenditures of effort in other areas, too. Promotion, education, networking, and the basic busywork business of doing business. We can't work 24/7. We have other obligations, other interests. Something is always pulling at us, trying to pry us away from our creative work which is the backbone and bread and butter of our writing business.

I work 9-to-5 and have for going on twelve years. When I wasn't working, I had two sons at home. I have family, friends, organizations, entertainments, illness and distractions just like the rest of you. And I've written over 50 books since the '80s. Not by whining about not having time. Not because I'm superwoman. But because I learned very early on how to make the most of any available time I had . . . because my time was money, and it was up to me how to spend it.

I'm talking about choices and their consequences.

I work at a law office. I'm at my desk from 9-to-5 with a half hour lunch, vacation and sick time. I put in my time and I get paid every other week. I have business I need to accomplish during those hours, and if I can't get it done, we don't make money when my boss goes to court. If I decided to get my nails filed rather than come in at 9, or linger for a two-and-a-half-hour lunch with my sister, or don't want to get wet walking from my apartment to the carport to go in that day so I stay home, those are my choices. And then come the consequences. Pretty simple, right?

I work as a writer. I'm at my desk from 5-to-8 AM every weekday and often from 6-to-3 Saturday and Sunday. I have business to accomplish during those hours, and if I don't get it done, I don't make any money when I miss my deadline or fail to turn in a new proposal. If I decide to sleep in or spend the weekend watching Netflix or shopping for shoes that will hurt my feet, or would rather go to see a game or a movie with friends or family, those are my choices. And then comes the consequence. Hmmm. Both are jobs, so why are we programmed to see the importance of one and not the other?

Are they so different? Both require effort and attendance. Both will result in a pink slip if you don't keep up with either of them. Yet we don't give our career in writing the same weight or value as we do our career as a legal assistant, a lab tech, a teacher, a stay-at-home-mom.

The fault lies in perception. We're self-employed. Our time is our own. We can make our own hours, show up when we want to and play fast and loose with our schedule. We know it and so does everyone else. The problem with this perception is, if we don't take our writing seriously, neither will the rest of the world. How can we expect others to respect our professional time if we make no set allowances for it? Hmmm. Food for thought.

We set up a budget for spending our money. We also need to set up a budget for spending our time.

Budgeting time when you're on contract is easy. You have an end date: your deadline. And you have so many days to reach it. Simple math (even if you don't DO math). How much time do you need to get your book done…realistically? How can you fit that length of time into the daily/weekly hours you have available to write? Create a schedule and stick to it. Just like budgeting your finances.

And just like your finances, stuff happens. Your car breaks down. Your daughter needs braces. Something is always siphoning off the money you expected to have. Your time is like that, too. Something always comes up. You have a meeting at school. You have a dentist appointment. Someone in your family is inconsiderate enough to have a birthday party. Choices. You have them with both your time and your money. Spend or save? Ask yourself do you NEED it, or do you just WANT it. That's the first criteria when spending. If it's a need, you usually just suck it up and do it. If it's a want, it's up to you to weigh its value against the consequence of losing time or money. You don't NEED to do everything that comes up any more than you NEED to buy everything that you see.

WHAT'S IN IT FOR ME?

Let's face it, you're often your own worst enemy. You have the power to control the time aspect of your career by your choices, but you're also a victim of it. By the very nature of being a published author, you become a go-to 'expert' in the field of writing. You're suddenly overwhelmed with requests from the public:

Could you judge in our contest? Could you speak at our conference? Could you sign at our store? Could you blog on my site? Could you write an article for our magazine? Could you send promotional items for our library? Could you mentor one of our unpublished authors? Could you critique for our fund raiser? Could we interview you for our newspaper article on Valentine's Day? Then there are the requests from your publisher: Could you set up a page on our community site and blog? Could you do a video interview? Could you sign up on Goodreads, Amazon, etc. and interact with readers? Could you? Yes. At first you want to say YES to everything. You're flattered, excited to be asked, eager to get out there and meet and greet. And soon, you're exhausted, burned out, and have sacrificed over half your writing time for the sake of others.

Then, at that point, it becomes a business necessity to weigh your options with the simple question of "What's in it for me?"

It sounds self-serving and selfish, but it's a business survival tool. You can't be everything to everybody, so you have to learn to evaluate the requests for your valuable time. And to say NO.

What's in it for me? This doesn't always mean the biggest bang for your buck. It could mean choosing something close to your heart. Or something vital to your career.

Here's a scale I use for placing value on my time:

1. I <u>have</u> to do it. No choice involved.
2. I <u>want</u> to do it if at all possible.
3. I'll <u>try</u> to do it if I can.

Assign each task a number and make no apologies or excuses.

1) I have to do it, so I do. I make whatever arrangements or adjustment necessary to make it so. These can be professional or personal obligations or opportunities. Pocket asks me to do some special extra content for the launch of their PocketAfterDark website. It means bringing my laptop to the RWA conference in Orlando to write up a Travel Diary to New Orleans around my other obligations. Will I do it? You bet. Do critiques for my Mid-Michigan RWA Chapter fundraiser and help fellow members? I do. Every year regardless of my deadlines.

2) I want to do it if at all possible. If I can get my work done early. If I can carve out another niche of time sometime later in the week to catch up. If I can't, maybe next time. Volunteer to judge in contests? I like to if I can. This year, yes, last year, no. Participate in your blog event? Yes, I think it's doable.

3) I'll try to do it if I can. No promises. It's a spur of the moment thing. Don't count on me. Attend a conference workshop? Stop by at a local signing? It depends on my schedule, how tired I am after I get out of the 9-to-5.

Don't make choices and not stand by them. That undermines the value you place on yourself and your time.

What's in it for me? Ask yourself these questions:

- Is it a stepping stone for my career? A unique situation that won't come again?
- Is the benefit more for the asker or for me? If I speak, is it to an audience that is interested in my product? Can I sell my books? If I blog, will it reach enough readers to justify the time? If I drive to an event across the state, will enough people show up to make the trip worthwhile (will they follow up with an article for the benefit of those who weren't there?)
- What kind of buzz can generate from my participation?
- Am I reaching a new audience, or am I preaching to the same choir?

- Can I afford to step away from my business of writing right now?

- Is it something I want to do because I enjoy it or believe in it strongly even if there's no measurable return? Yes, I will write a column in our chapter newsletter to support our published authors. Yes, I will donate time or books to support a cause.

- Will anyone miss me if I don't show up?

- Will my grandson ever turn four again? My critique partner retire? My son play in his first band concert or his first Little League game? Parent teacher conferences? Those are no brainers. Wouldn't miss them for the world.

- Am I getting reimbursed for my time and money spent? Are they offering a speaker's fee, a discount on the conference, free room and mileage, payment for the article?

- Can I enrich my career, my profession, my livelihood, my wellbeing by attending?

- Will I lose sales if I don't post on Facebook or Twitter or my blog today?

What's in it for me? That answer is unique to you and your current situation. Don't undervalue your time or overestimate the importance of saying yes to every request. But remember, you can't earn a living if you're not actively in pursuit of it.

Sometimes, it's not all about you. We often mistakenly believe that we have to do everything ourselves and thereby dilute our valuable time with business that could easily be done by someone else. When you're in charge of your career, it's difficult to know when and what to delegate. Sometimes paying someone else to do a task for you frees you up to do something more important. It takes time and money and effort to learn a new trick when there are others out there who have that expertise already. Which is more cost effective? To take the time away from your writing to research, design, set up and maintain your blog (presuming you have the skills already to even attempt the task), or is it cheaper to have someone manage it for you? Don't be too prideful, too particular or too embarrassed to ask for help when you need it. Have a family member attach those tassels on your bookmark. Ask a co-worker to drop something off at the post office for you. Have someone come in to clean your tubs and toilet. Ask your mom to watch the kids for an afternoon a week to give you some private writing time. Hire a virtual assistant to take care of all those time-sucking tasks you don't have time to do.

If you delegate, do it smartly. Think about it if you don't have the time, energy or expertise to do it yourself, if it's more cost-effective to farm it out than to learn it if you're on an impossible deadline, or if it creates unbearable stress that's diminishing the quality of your work.

And it's a write off.

Pick the best person for the job, remembering that the most expensive isn't always the best. Get references and check out samples of their work. Be very clear on what you need them to do, what you're using it for, and when you need it, and make sure you provide them with all the necessary materials. Have them send you a preview for your final approval.

Keep track of how and where and on what you spend your allotted writing time. That's the best way to discover if you're spending it wisely or wasting it without being aware of it. Are you spending most of your available writing time checking e-mail, playing Spider Solitaire or surfing the web? Do Twitter and FaceBook own you? Are you working on your next blog post instead of Chapter Five? Are you distracted by phone calls, unexpected company, by the arrival of the mailman?

You could probably make your own chart and note times and activities, but I'm all about tech tools these days, so here are some fun and fabulous products that keep track of the clock so you don't have to:

- Google calendar: Like Microsoft Explorer calendar and Outlook calendar, it offers multiple calendars so you can track business(es) and personal events separately or overlay them. They sync with mobile devices and can send text and e-mail reminders. I used Outlook calendar to keep a diary of what I did while researching in New Orleans which was wonderfully helpful in creating that blog diary, and to justify my expenses.

- TaDa Lists: A free app where you can subscribe to various types of lists for chores, events, etc. with access to your mobile devices, and can be shared with others.

- Action Method: This one is an intriguing project manager that controls your to-dos, projects, events, and deadlines. It has Focus to help you prioritize, an Advisor that charts your productivity, and Project Notes so you can jot down details. The IPad app I'm going to be checking out is $1.99.

- Manic Time: This free download is a time-tracking program that monitors what you're doing on your computer and charts it so you can see how much of your day is REALLY spent on Social Media and Solitaire.

- Ink Link: This program tracks the submission process for each manuscript or article, shows how much time you spend on each one, where they're been sent, how long they've been there and what the result was, creates a resume of your published work and a financial report of your writing-related income and expenses. It also generates follow-up letters for the status of your projects.

Writing is a business. YOUR business. Time is money. Spend it wisely.

Summary:

1. Set up a Business Plan to govern your writing career.
2. Make keeping accurate financial records a priority.
3. Figure out your monthly expenses to find your base income. This is the least amount you can

get by on to cover your bills and other obligations

4. Average your income to reflect the minimum monthly intake to offset fluctuations.

5. Pay yourself a set salary by withdrawing only that amount.

6. Save any excess or bonus after the deduction of salary.

7. Keep income after expenses in the positive not the negative by adjusting your spending with an emphasis on needs not wants.

8. Have an emergency savings account to cover at least three months of your expenses.

9. Establish a budget that includes payment of expenses, savings and taxes of 28% on your writing income (after deduction of writing expenses). If you can meet it for over six months, or better yet, a year, you're ready to become a full-time, self-supporting writer.

10. Writing is your business. Your time IS money. Make your decisions accordingly.

Getting It Out There: PR and Social Media For Writers

blogging

interviews

twitter

facebook

BRANDING: What's In a Name?

Award-Winning Author

Nancy Gideon

Branding: - What's in a Name?

What is Branding?

The publishing industry loves its buzz words. A few years ago, they had authors puzzling over the meaning of "High Concept." It was a nightmare trying to figure out what the "High Concept" of your manuscript was when no one had an exact definition for the term. Now the go-to phrase that has everyone scurrying is "Branding." Other than the rather wince-inducing S&M connotations, what exactly does it mean when you brand yourself as an author?

A Brand is all about identity, a way to quickly alert the public to who you are and what you offer.

In the old days, a Brand was a way to identify an item or service being offered to a largely illiterate public: the mortar and pestle of the druggist, the striped pole or shears for the barber, a tooth for the dentist, a symbol burned into the hide of horses and cattle to identify their owner. Think of the highway signs you look forward to seeing on the side of the road indicating restaurant, gas and a place to sleep. Smart advertisers jumped on the branding bandwagon to get their products instantly recognized: Apple, Windows, the NBC peacock and CBS eye, the elephant and donkey in the political ring, right down to the stick figures on restroom doors and number of stars next to your hotel. Consumers want to know immediately what they're getting and the quicker the seller can assure them that they've come to the right place to meet that need, the better the chance of making a connection.

Your author brand, simply put, is the impact and reputation you build in the industry that tells the reader exactly what to expect when they see your name. It's the image, perception or identity that you purposefully create to set you apart from the others in your vast field, one that readers will recognize at a glance. Branding is about name recognition and recall. Your brand will do three things: 1) create an emotional bond between you and the reader based on loyalty and trust, 2) position you and your books through the use of awards, reviews and word of mouth as a go-to for high quality, which immediately brings more attention, and 3) establishes your own personal statement that sets you apart from the crowd through your unique author Voice and style.

Branding for a writer is multi-faceted. You're creating an author brand that relays who you are as a writer, and a book brand which determines how your book is going to be portrayed to the public, how it fits in the market, and how it's sold. Which comes first, the author or the book? <u>The author</u>. The purpose of branding is to get the reader to follow you as an author throughout your career, not for just one book. It's not about selling books. It's about selling yourself.

Why is author branding necessary?

If you're like me, you became a writer because you HAD to write. You couldn't NOT write. It was all about those words on the page, that sense of magic as your story unfolds. The last thing you want is one more time suck to keep you from the computer, especially to wrestle with something as innocuous as branding.

Over the years, I've developed a rather selfish shell to protect my writing time. I call it WIIFM: What's in it for me? My local and national writers' organizations may be non-profit, but I consider writing a business, a career, and I'm definitely profit-based. That doesn't mean I don't do philanthropic things. But the bottom line is the bottom line. Do I volunteer my time to help others? Yes, I do. Would I write without pay? You bet I would, and I have. But the joy of writing doesn't pay my rent. My advances and royalties do. So if something is going to get in the way of my hands on keys, I need to know how it's going to benefit me in the long run.

What's In It For Me?

Let me be very clear about what proper branding can do for you.

- Branding builds your readership
- It helps potential readers find you
- It lets readers know what they're getting so they won't be disappointed (and if you disappoint them, you don't usually get a second chance)
- Branding pumps up your social media efforts so that less is more, and you have more time to write
- It helps you determine your market niche so you can target it more effectively without wasting time and money chasing after an audience who is not interested in what you offer
- Strong branding shows agents and editors that you have a savvy promotional platform that can translate into sales and a long, profitable future, which is what's in it for <u>them</u>.

A smart author looking to build the foundation of a long career needs to start thinking of their potential readership as a marketing group and of their book writing as a business. That author needs to be ready to spend as much time and energy with the marketing of the product as in creating it.

A naïve author asks, "But isn't that what a publishing house is supposed to do for me?" Maybe in a perfect world, but in the real world authors are expected to do the majority of their own book promotion. Fiction writers need to learn a little something from their non-fiction brethren who routinely add the marketing element into their initial book proposals by identifying their market, their target audience, their positioning in the marketplace, and what makes their product unique, but also commercial. Most fiction writers don't take that into consideration until after the book is finished

An ever tightening market has forced writers to justify the purchase of their books, not only to the editor, but to the marketing, sales, and accounting departments. Don't be surprised if you're asked "Who do you write like?" and "What other books out there are like yours?" Of course, you want to say that you're a complete original, but that's not the answer they're looking for. Publishers want to know where you belong in the grand scheme of things. They want to know where you'll fit into their catalog, how their marketing machine is going to sell you to their accounts, and where to place your and who will buy you on the shelves. That author brand you create for yourself will provide those answers. That strong author brand will convince buyers to pick you instead of the books on either side of you and build reader loyalty that will parlay into more sales, bigger and better contracts, and industry recognition because you stand out next to competing brands. In effect, and I shudder to say it, your author brand is more important than the content of your book and its packaging when it comes to sales.

Say it ain't so! What could be more powerful than your words? Ask any publishing icon: Stephen King, Nora Roberts, Tom Clancy, James Patterson, Sue Grafton, Janet Evanovich. Their names sell their next books before the public reads a single word, or even has a glimpse of the cover. They don't look for that new book by the title. They look for the new Dan Brown or Lisa Gardner.

Do unpublished authors need an author brand?

Before you could sell your books to the public, you'd have to sell them to an agent or a publisher. Even if you skip the tradition middle men and opt to go to digital on you own, you still need to create a way to stand out amongst the tens of thousands that have made that same choice on the month of your new release. Good writing isn't enough. You need someone to read your work for it to get that positive buzz going. Having that darn fine book isn't a guarantee that it will stick if you just throw it up on the Ethernet wall. If you've prepared the way in advance with smart promotion and strong author branding, you have a far greater chance that an editor or a browsing buyer will be ready to take a chance on you, especially when you're a debut author.

Think of editors as the way you would the HR department in a corporation. If they're considering your work, you can bet they've searched your name on the Internet to see what comes up. Which do you want them to see: No matches found, or a professional presence that conveys your carefully crafted message? They're not looking for temp workers. They're looking for a long term investment that will pay off with as little training as possible.

When agents and publishers evaluate your first book proposal, they want to know that you'll be able to successfully promote that package. To convince them that you can effectively and confidently market that product, authors need to start building their author platform as soon as they embark on a publishing career. That platform determines an author's visibility, their appeal to a potential readership and their impact in the marketplace. And the best time to begin construction is before you begin the book.

Building your author platform

Regardless of where you are in your publishing journey, whether you're just taking your first steps, whether you've hit a comfortable stride, or you're cruising in high style, you should continue to develop, strengthen and fine tune your author platform. Your platform includes your Internet presence, your publishing credits, your public appearances, your awards and any other method you might use to get and hold the attention of your readership. Creating that platform is crucial to the success of a new author, or even for established authors reinventing themselves.

An author platform consists of a powerhouse trifecta: Your unique brand, your reputation as a consistent quality writer, and the network of connections you've made that will further your career. Creating your author brand is the foundation of that platform.

Building anything substantial that's made to last requires a blueprint, a roadmap, a plan. You need to decide who you are as an author, and how you'll define yourself and your books to the buying public.

Deciding on your Brand

It's all about <u>YOU</u>.

Not your first book. Not your next book. Not your career.

Unlike any other commercial business, writing is different because <u>YOU</u> are the product you're promoting. Branding is the process of consistently conveying your unique qualities across multiple far-reaching outlets so that they become recognizable. Personal branding isn't hype or bragging. It's about discovering what you excel in then focusing on those genuine attributes to build or re-invent your career.

Finding your brand is like recognizing your own unique author's Voice. The success of your brand depends upon how accurately it represents you and how well it translates the unique YOU to the marketplace. To be successful, it has to be believable.

When I was doing a guest blog Q&A, some of the unexpectedly pointed questions made me pause and think: What five attributes would you use to best describe yourself? How do other people describe you? As I answered each question, I realized that some of the responses were exact opposites. The way I saw myself was not the same way I was perceived. How could both views be correct without the perception being confused?

Ask yourself right now:

- What five attributes would you use to best describe yourself?
- How do other people describe you?

Write those answers down and compare them. Do they match up or are you looking at two completely different people?

You can be unintentionally branded by the impressions you project without even being aware of it. Sometimes these can be negative traits—unapproachable, prima donna, bitchy, hard to work with, unreliable, inconsistent, sloppy—that are picked up accidently: from a scowling photo, from a refusal to respond to e-mails, from a failure to follow through on an expectation, from an amateurish or seldom updated website. It's up to you as an author to project strong, positive images and consistently reinforce them.

Having a successful brand means you've focused on an image that resonates in people's minds when they think of you. That image should reflect your unique qualities that set you apart from everyone else. Many authors confuse brand with image. They're not the same thing. Image plays a large part in the establishment of your brand. It's created from the perceptions others have of you: your appearance, your clothing choices, your attitude, even your language. These perceptions should complement each other, not conflict. For example, you wouldn't expect a hard-boiled crime author who is an ex-marine to be overly emotional, have butterfly wallpaper on his website and feature canning recipes, or to find your favorite inspirational author in a bar wearing scanty attire dishing profanely on her latest affair. You need to make sure your message isn't confusing, so keep it as authentic as possible. If a reader feels betrayed or tricked by the image you project, how can they trust you not to disappoint them in other areas?

Start your branding quest by asking yourself who you are as an author. Make a list.

- What do you want to write? Blockbusters? Feel good books? Thrillers? Jump out of your seat horror? How-tos? Coming of age? Urban fantasy?

- What kind of writer do you want to be seen as? Edgy? Comedic? Profound? Prolific? Satirist? Poetic? A thorough researcher? An expert in your area? Break all the rules or commercial?

- Who will be reading your books? Tweenagers? Senior citizens? The moral right or radical left? Blue or white collar? Stay-at-home Moms? Gamers or Geeks?

- What main ingredients are found in your books? Suspense? Humor? Gritty language? Graphic violence? Plot twists? Family values? Life lessons? Bedroom door open or closed?

- Where would your books be shelved in a bookstore? Romance? Fantasy? Action/Adventure? Young Adult? Mystery?

The answers to the above should help you find your publishing niche, the place you'll fit in the current marketplace. To sell you, a publisher has to know how to categorize you. To buy you, a reader needs to be able to find you by searching for specific words or tags that fit their interests. And your brand has to fulfill their expectations. You are your most important product, so position yourself carefully. Your brand needs to be able to grow with your career, with you as a writer and as a person.

How you target your brand, that defining niche, will determine how the public interacts with you. To be effective, your personal brand must be 1) tightly focused; 2) consistent; and, 3) accurately reflect the subject matter.

What's in a name?

Your name is your brand. You'll want to use it exclusively across all your promotional outlets instead of picking cutesy nicknames for your Twitter account. You'll want your website URL to be your name, as well as your blog and your e-mail addresses. Repetition reinforces name recognition, making it easier for readers to link all your efforts together.

Your own name or a pseudonym?

Here are some reasons for preferring to use a pen name:

1. To disguise gender. Who knew the sensual historical romances of Jennifer Wilde were actually written by Tom Huff, that Leigh Greenwood was a Southern gentleman named Lee, or science fiction author Andre Norton was really Mary Alice?

2. To distinguish between different genres. So as not to confuse her romance readers, Nora Roberts penned her harder-edged futuristic cop series as J.D. Robb. Jayne Ann Krentz (contemporary romantic suspense)/Jayne Castle (futuristic)/Amanda Quick (historical) books are all distinguished by different tones and genres.

3. To fit genre expectations. As an iconic western author, Zane Gray dropped his

real given name of Pearl to use his middle name.

4. <u>To sound more glamorous, less (or more) ethnic or easier to remember.</u> Irving Wallechinsky became Irving Wallace, which was far easier to spell and pronounce. Kathy Grill chose the name Jade Lee to compliment her Asian heritage and the exotic characters and locales of her romances. F. Scott creates a more worldly and dashing image than Francis Fitzgerald.

5. <u>To protect the privacy of the author's personal life</u>. If your background is teaching, ministry or public office, you might not want to be outted as the author of erotic romances, or if you've written a sensitive expose, tell-all or satire, having your identity known could jeopardize your career.

6. <u>To put more books out.</u> If you're a prolific writer, a pen name allows you to have more titles on the shelves without gutting the market and diluting your impact.

7. <u>If you write for more than one publishing house.</u> It once was common practice for publishers to insist that you write under a

pseudonym that they could legally own and build exclusively.

8. <u>To recover from bad numbers or a bad impression.</u> If your books have failed to live up to market expectations for whatever reason, your agent or publisher may suggest you take on a pseudonym to rebuild your career with a fresh start.

Whether it's your name or a nom de plume, before you invest time and money into creating your brand around it, check to see if it's in use by another author by searching Google, whitepages.com and the Amazon database. If your name is James Patterson, use your middle name and go for James Thomas or J. Thomas Patterson. If you were born Sue Smith consider using your maiden name of Breckenridge or modify it to Suzette Smythe. Remember, branding is all about making your name memorable and unique. It's hard to stand out if you're one of a dozen William Stevensons. Pick a name that you'll be comfortable with, one that resonates with you and your writing niche, then own it.

Identifying your brand

Once you've decided on a name, you'll want to personalize your brand, to make it reflect the qualities readers can consistently find in your work, and the characteristics that will make them want to connect with you. What keywords can you attach to your brand that describe its feel, its audience, and its appeal? Once you've identified your genre niche and your writing style, here are some other defining factors that target your market with an emotional response to you, as the author and your author brand:

- <u>Geographical ties</u>: the Deep South, the West, East versus West Coast, the Heartland to the Highlands, urban or tropical jungle. Hit them where they live or dream of living.

- <u>Shared characteristics</u>: What things about you can the reader relate to? What traits or experiences of yours are amplified in your books? Are you or do you write about the Baby Boomers, Gen-X or Gen-Y? Are you a Wall Street wizard or a Wiccan, a former marine, a lawyer, a priest, a detective, the victim of a violent crime or survivor of a tragedy? A single mom or a self-made entrepreneur? A trauma nurse or a grief counselor?

- <u>Series or recurring characters</u>: Can you say <u>Harry Potter</u> or <u>Dark Hunters</u>? Miss Marple, Stephanie Plum, Alex Cross or Cat and Bones?

- <u>Celebrity comparisons:</u> Are you the Paris Hilton of Honolulu? The Paula Dean of Pittsburgh? The next Dave Barry or Jackie Collins?

- <u>Credentials:</u> *New York Times* or *US Today* bestseller, a PhD, an award or prize winner? Establishing yourself as an expert or as someone who is recognized as outstanding in your field immediately commands attention.

Pick one of the above or combine them to create images and associations that will make readers seek you out. Think Southern Vampire Mysteries. That's a one-two-three punch tying in a trio of powerful identifiers that worked quite well for Charlaine Harris. Remember, your brand is like your author resume. It's only important if it's relevant to what you're trying to project. The fact that you have a degree in ancient religions is noteworthy if you're writing the next Dan Brown series, but not so much if your niche is children's books. The fact that you're a dentist isn't part of your brand unless the heroine in your suspense series is involved in solving a crime through forensic dentistry.

Getting Started

You've asked and answered the important questions regarding your brand:

1) <u>How you want to be known</u>. Think of those icons and what words you associate with them: Stephen King-horror, Robert Ludlum-action thrillers, Agatha Christie-mystery, Deepak Chopra- transcendental self-help, Lisa Gardner-suspense, Georgette Heyer-regency romance, Arthur Agatston M.D.-health/diet, Ray Bradbury-science fiction, Cassandra Clare-young adult

2) <u>What image you want to project.</u> Are you jeans or designer dress? Tomboy or debutant? Funny or serious? Hard-edged or romantic? Dark or bright? Fixer-upper or 5-star?

3) <u>Your genre niche.</u> Steampunk, Menage, How-to, Chick Lit, cozy mystery, adventure, fantasy, Scottish historical, BDSM, police procedural.

4) <u>Your target audience</u>. Over 50, under 15, single professionals, crafty moms, the eclectic, the escapist, the thrill seeker, the Gone Green, the intellectual.

Now it's time to get the basics ready to launch your brand.

Branding: - What's in a Name?

Establishing a brand doesn't mean you need an expensive logo, an extensive back list or a tech professional designing your spaces. It means you have to have a focused image and target words associated with YOU that will get the attention and stick in the memory of the reading public. Unpublished authors often make the mistake of setting up a domain and website hype around an unsold book before building an author brand. Branding a book, alone, before it's set for publication is never a good idea because you don't know how the publisher and its marketing department is going to present the finished product. You may have it branded as an edgy suspense only to have the cover flash calling it a Secret Baby story. You can't always convince your publisher to come on board with your ideas and concepts. If you've worked your Social Media up to include specific colors and images that are soft and pastel then the released product comes out in stark graphics and bold red, your pre-efforts at branding are wasted. And the chance of them keeping that original title, no matter how well you've 'branded' it, are iffy at best. You do need a good product, but your first job is working on your marketing strategy: Who you are, where you fit into the marketplace, and why readers should want to connect with you. This is true even if you're self-publishing because you're in it for the long haul, not the one title, and if New York comes calling and picks up your book, then changes the title and the marketing concept, you're back to the beginning. You want your author platform to be built on the one variable you can control: YOU. From that platform, you can market not only your current book, but all your books and accomplishments, past, present and future, even if they're not with the same publisher.

These are the basics you need to have in place before launching your author brand . . . even before you think about putting your book out there.

Author photo

You want to put a face on your brand. Readers like to feel they're relating to a real person. You'll want to invest in a professional looking photo you can use to build recognition. This doesn't have to be a studio headshot, but can also be a posed shot in a specific setting. Remember, the key word is professional. If you use a picture taken on a cell phone of you standing in your backyard dappled by shadows from your tulip tree, the image it creates is not going to be very favorable. I would strongly suggest an experienced photograph who can make the best of light and shadows . . . and can airbrush away those flyaway strands of hair, whiten your teeth and firm your chin. A good photographer will NOT make you look like someone you're not by erasing all your well-earned character lines or allow you to pack on a ton of cosmetics that sit unnaturally on your face. You want you...the best YOU you can be, not an artificial mask. You don't want readers to come up to you and exclaim that you look nothing like your picture (so no using that 20-year-old wedding photo or the overly dramatic glamor shot).

Enhance your brand using the level of formality, your clothing, color, and background to reflect the image you want to project. If you write crime novels, you might want to have an urban backdrop with a gritty, stark quality, have your pose authoritative, and perhaps leather-clad. If your brand centers around home and hearth, you might pick a cozy interior setting with fireplace, pet, relaxed yarn sweater and jeans to amplify that casual, approachable feel. Paranormal authors can play with fantasy backgrounds with wisps of smoke, intriguing shadow and genre appropriate clothing (not necessarily costuming—you don't want to go too over the top). If you write historical westerns, you can opt for chunky turquoise jewelry and ramp it up with western attire to whatever degree you feel comfortable. Or you can choose a strictly professional studio portrait with anything from a soft haloing light and pastel backdrop to a variety of settings from woods to bookshelves or dramatic angular black and white. Look for examples of what others have used that you think reflects the image you want to establish and let your photograph know the mood you're trying to capture.

When I was attending the national romance writers' conference in Washington, D.C., I made an appointment to have professional promotional photos taken. They ones I'd been using were old black & whites taken by a local photographer, and I needed something updated, color and digital. I got my hair professionally styled the way I usually wore it—only with about four pounds of spray to make sure it stayed put. The day you get your pictures, is not the time to experiment with a new cut, color or arrangement. I selected two outfits: one a professional suit jacket with bold accessories and a top with slightly more casual lines to reflect a relaxed image. I keep both in warm neutral tones that complemented my coloring and the color palette I was planning for my promotional materials. I had several dozen shots taken with different backgrounds, lens and lighting and immediately was able to select the three I wanted. My photographer took off twenty pounds (bless his heart!), brightened my smile and the whites of my eyes, eliminated just a few of my lines and any strands that managed to escape that shellac of hair products on those three poses. We went over package options and I chose to have just the single set of proofs and a digital copy. Make sure you get the rights to reproduce the photos. The photographer will often require you to list a photo credit. It was quick, not horrendously expensive and I had my primary branding tool ready for use.

Whatever you pick, make sure it's an accurate interpretation of your brand, something that you can use across multiple social networks, on your book jacket, and in your press kit to gain recognition and connect to readers on an emotional, personal level. Wherever you put your photo, provide your name and tagline as a caption along with photo credit if required.

Author Bio

Your bio is your next most important image asset. It's a thumbnail introduction to your author platform: who you are and what you write. This is the place for you to define your image, expand your tagline, list your credentials and connect to your social media. This is NOT a place to put anything without direct and focused reference to your brand. Create a long and a short version to suit the situation. The long version would go on your About page on your website where you have the luxury of length to tuck in expanded details, and the short version is for the About Me spots on your book jacket, publisher page, Facebook, Twitter, blog, Google, Author Central and beneath any article your write. Always sync your bio with your photo.

Your author bio will contain the basic facts of your author platform: your name, your tagline niche, and the reason readers should take notice of you i.e. New York Times bestseller, Nebula or Prism winner, former Congressional aide, syndicated columnist, 30-year veteran of the police force, foster mother to over 200 abused children. As space allows, you can update those facts to include your relevant current title, speaking engagement, cause, etc. keeping relevant in mind. And don't forget a link to your website. Never waste an opportunity to lead a potential reader to where they can get more information about you.

Taglines

Another important part of your brand that makes you stand out and memorable is your tagline. A tagline is a short, catchy phrase. This single bullet point that tells the reader in a glance who you are and what you do, goes after your name in promotional materials.

Branding: - What's in a Name?

Your brand might stay the same over the course of your career but a tagline can change as long as it still amplifies your brand. You can create a new tagline for each book or series or with the addition of a new marketing level: #1 NYT bestseller, debut or launch author, Edgar winner, etc.

A tagline has a very specific job to do in a short space. It's your identifier and your sales pitch. Your tagline should do the following things in order to be effective:

1. Reflect and enhance your author brand
2. Be memorable and easily identifiable as your own
3. Should be unique and not too similar to someone else's
4. Extends a promise that you as an author will keep

Advertisers have always used taglines to support the brand they're selling to the public. You should recognize them immediately: Coke, It's the Real thing, Staples, That was Easy, Nationwide, It's on your side, Allstate, You're in good hands, McDonalds', i'm loving it, Mercedes-Benz, the best or nothing, Lowe's, Let's build something together. Each of these slogans promise something to the consumer. So should our taglines. Here are just a few I've found when scrolling through my e-mail:

- Teresa Wilde, **Handcuffed to the Sheikh:** Best. Abduction. Ever
- Alice Coleman, Romance, Paranormal & Urban Fantasy—Love Beyond Human Boundaries
- Jeffrey Deaver, Master of the Mind Game
- Jessa Slade, Love Conquers All . . . Which explains the scars
- Shobhan Bantwal, Experience "Bollywood in a Book"
- Lisa Gardner, #1 *New York Times* bestselling author of suspense
- Arianna Skye, A Dash of Snark Meets Dark
- Ashley Chase, Where There's Fire, There's Ash
- Arthur Agatston, M.D., Author of the *New York Times* bestseller *The South Beach Diet*
- Bethany House, the Top Name in Inspiration Historical Fiction

Visual Impact

Your brand should have an individual feel or tone, something that makes it uniquely yours and, again, supports your overall brand. Your choice of visual details gives the reader an immediate emotional response that is powerful and consistent with your brand. These same details, when applied across your promotional print and social media outlets creates a unifying impression.

Color, font and graphics all convey your brand at a glance. A horror author wouldn't have pastels, flowers and curlicue lettering on his business cards any more than a sweet romance writer would choose blood-dripping font and images of handcuffs and police tape. Those inconsistencies would completely confuse . . . and lose a potential reader. Each layering detail needs to add to and build upon your chosen brand.

- Western author: earth tones > strong serif fonts > images synonymous with cowboys, the desert, Native American symbols
- Steampunk author: gritty urban tones > techie, unique fonts > gears, machines, industrial images
- Mystery/suspense series: dark backgrounds with bold slashes of color > big, boldly colored text > stark, heavily shadowed graphics featuring a single image i.e. apprehensive eyes, partially opened doorway, or a weapon

- Comedy/Chick Lit: Bright colors > fancy fonts > carefree images or cartoon caricatures
- Medical thrillers: clinical colors like white, silver, reflective glass and metallic surfaces > thin precise lettering > sharp, sterile images like an operating theater, overturned gurney, scalpel, hospital hallway

When applying your visual elements, think display case rather than flea market table. You don't want to dilute the impact with clutter that makes the reader work to pick out your intentions. The impression should be clean, clear and eye-catching.

Logos

Your logo is the simple graphic that's used to represent you and the message behind your brand. When placed on your business cards, your website, and your printed materials and even used in your signature line, it represents your brand in a way that's simple and memorable. It can be your photo or a graphic that repeats the colors and other emotional elements you've already established. It needs to be easily resized without losing clarity and something you can use over a long period of time without losing relevance. Bloggers have become very creative and clever with the use of a logo that conveys the tone and emphasis of their site at a glance using a stiletto heel, champagne glass, vampire fangs, and a budding rose on a beach, a white collar with a red lipstick print, handcuffs, a bare torso and pair of tight jeans.

A logo should consolidate the feel of who you are and what you represent without being specific, i.e. using a particular book cover. But, like a tagline, you can create a logo that unites a series AND reinforces your brand. Sherrilyn Kenyon has been particularly successful with her Dark Hunter series, tying them together with a double bow symbol that instantly identifies them on everything from her website to her book covers. Cindy Arends has created a slinky devil in a red dress to represent her Sidney Ayers's Sinful Snarky Paranormal Romance on her blog and website, and uses it to differentiate that brand from her other pen name that deals with erotic romance. American West historical author Rosanne Bittner developed a fitting Heart of the West logo using a heart shaped outline to replace the word heart.

Simple is better and when using color, it can be bright, but don't make it so dazzling or busy that it distracts from the message.

Online Author Brand

Your online impact starts with a website. From there, all other social media outlets are like satellite offices carrying the same brand message, all linking to that central site. The key word is consistency.

To effectively create an online presence make sure you follow these guidelines:

- Sync your photo and bio on all your online avenues for quick reader identification
- Utilize the same color palette, fonts, graphics and logo on every service. Work your logo into your blog and Twitter background.
- Link, link, link. Tie everything together so readers can skip from one outlet to the next without having to search. Set up a Contact page or use sidebars or footers so visitors can navigate quickly throughout your author platform.
- Establish the same screen name for all online services. Get your domain as your name, if possible and use that name or something similar for e-mail, blog, Facebook, Twitter, etc. so readers can find you more easily
- Your professional social media efforts should be focused only on that brand. You need to keep your family and friends separate to target your audience interest and effectiveness.
- Direct your content toward your brand niche and keep it updated and fresh so readers will return frequently.

- Follow through with personal contacts. Answer your e-mails, respond to comments, and leave comments on other social networks. Be approachable and reliable.

- Connect with others in your same niche. Join blog and writer loops, follow similar blogs and see who they follow. Add those who follow you to tighten the network.

For Example

Excellent examples of author branding are JoAnn Ross, Cassandra Clare and James Patterson.

When JoAnn Ross's Special Ops heroes took a turn from danger and suspense to recovery and reestablishing home ties, the author did a dramatic rebrand. Her uber-abbed High Risk series focus segued into Shelter Bay with calming coastal scenes, wide verandas and a coming home feeling that surfaced in an all new website and Facebook author page.

Cassandra Clare maintains the same young adult appeal through two separate websites that tie back into her own. Both her Mortal Instrument paranormal series and her Infernal Devices steampunk series are completely developed yet retain the same brand through tone, color, and style, and over-arcing author presence.

James Patterson is his own strong brand. On his clean, information-driven site, he neatly organizes all his series whether Maximum Ride or Alex Cross with the same format, offering character details and plot summations and various social media options from book trailers to his imbedded Facebook page. All professional, all Patterson and all around effective.

All three authors are audience aware, extremely proactive with social media, providing updates, additional content, and personal attention without compromising the consistency of their brand.

Branding Mistakes

Author branding isn't an exact science. It's a learn-as-you-go growing experience that can suffer growing pains. It can take up to four or more books to establish a reader base.

You'll need to adjust and tweak and expand as your career changes. The important thing is building with consistency to establish your brand, develop your readership and to meet their expectations.

There are several areas where you'll want to tread with care to avoid developing bad branding habits. Here are some to keep your eye on:

- Not being consistent. Talk the talk and walk the walk. Don't confuse and alienate readers by sending mixed signals

- Buy my book! Buy my book! Buy my book! The hard-sell doesn't make sales. It's about connecting with the readers on topics other than sales and self-promotion (which is the BEST kind of self-promotion). Give them extra content, test them with quizzes, do surveys, respond to their comments. Be interactive, not just in their face.

- Getting overwhelmed by trying to do everything yourself. This leads to failure to follow through and missed opportunities. Give yourself a break. Join a group niche-related blog or website where all the pressure doesn't rest on your shoulders alone. Hire a virtual assistant to help you prioritize, organize and wrestle with the tech details. Don't confuse quantity with quality.

- Fail to have a plan. Scattershot promotion is hit or miss. Failure to focus and follow through wastes time and breaks the promises you make to your readers.

- Doing too much or too little. This applies to both self-promotion and online time.

- Lacking confidence. Distancing yourself from your product because you're afraid of too much public attention, and fear of failure, rejection or ridicule.

- Having unrealistic expectations. It takes time to build a readership, to get visitors to your blog and friends on your social media pages. Don't give up too soon or jump to something else you think might net a faster result. You'll lose any momentum you might have gained.

- Over-staying in your comfort zone. Everything's working. That doesn't mean it's time to kick back and relax. It's often a sign it's time to update and upgrade to heighten interest and keep things fresh.

Summary - How to Build a Strong Author Brand

1. YOU are your brand. Decide what makes you unique.

2. Connect with your audience. Create an emotional response.

3. Build your brand using the same elements across all media whether online or print, spoken or visual.

4. Be consistent in marketing your brand so there's no confusion. Stick to your brand image and deliver so your readership won't be disappointed.

5. Continue to build, reevaluate and evolve so your brand keeps pace and accurately reflects your career.

Branding: - What's in a Name?

About the Author

Since 1987, award winning romance author, Nancy Gideon, has penned over 60 novels. She has written under the pseudonyms of Lauren Giddings, Dana Ransom, and Rosalyn West. She even writes screenplays and worked as an extra in one of the movies!

Her career has spanned the entire romance spectrum. Some would say she has helped push the once stifling boundaries of the genre to where they are today.

"A one of a kind author who leaves us begging for more!" The Literary Times,

"Readers will be mesmerized by her magical characters!" Romantic Times

"Tremendous novels full of action, romance and incredible characters. Nobody does a hero as well!" Affaire de Coeur

Gideon, Ransom, Giddings, by any other name...romance. We are proud to have acquired Nancy's professional musings on the business of writing.

To read more about Nancy and her work visit her Website at

http://www.nancygideon.com

or her Blog at

http://nancygideon.blogspot.com

www.ingramcontent.com/pod-product-compliance
Lightning Source LLC
Chambersburg PA
CBHW071440210326
41597CB00020B/3885